Psalms and Sorceries

Psalms and Sorceries

Wade German

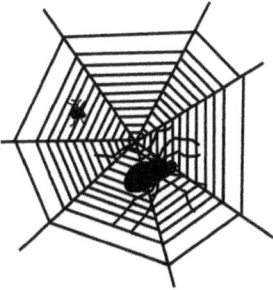

Hippocampus Press

New York

Contents

Nightscapes 7

    Rune 9

    Cernunnos 10

    Druidry 11

    The Ghosts of Hyperborea 12

    Out of Endor 13

    Ecclesiastical Triptych 14

       I. Relics 14

      II. Black Robes 15

     III. Ladies of the Everlasting Lichen 16

    The Shrine 17

    Alastor 18

    Oracle 19

    Spells 20

    Bats 21

    Toads 22

    Night Hags 23

    Hex House 24

    The Driver of the Dragon's Coach 25

    The Secret Prayer of Victor Frankenstein 26

Prophecies and Dooms 27

    The Nightmares 29

    Two Songs from The King in Yellow 33

       I. Naotalba's Dream Song 33

      II. "And All the Black Mould Sings" 34

    Prophecy of the Green Death 35

Fields of the Nephilim 37

Destroyers 39

The Sayings of the Seers 40

Haunted Planet 41

The Tomb of Wilum Hopfrog Pugmire 42

Lore 43

Occult Agency 46

Beddoes: Marginalia in a Cadaveric Atlas 47

Wraiths 48

Methuselah 49

Philomathes and Epistemon 50

The Monstrous Voice **55**

Scylla and Charybdis 57

Eurynomos 61

Gorgonum Chaos; or, The Sisters of Medusa 65

Children of Hypnos **71**

Acknowledgments **119**

Nightscapes

Rune

Now evening enters without sound
And banishes the noise of day.
In sudden silence, vast, profound,
An incommunicable name
Is uttered at night's portal way
Through which the shadow world evolves,
And spectral entities reclaim
The kingdom that the day dissolves.

Emerald moons and stars emerge
Above silentious land below
Where darkness reigns as demiurge,
Whose worship demon, ghoul, and witch
Attend as acolytes who know
The very silence is a rune—
A psalm of seances, by which
The shadows of the world commune.

Cernunnos

I was before the oldest stars were born;
Across the eons has my shadow loomed.
Though many names and shapes have I assumed,
A crown of antlers I have always worn—
And nighted, wooded hills have been my fane
Since long before the Neolithic age—
When secret covens, led by witch and mage,
Evolved to keep my rite, that I remain,
And grant my evil, everlasting boon:
Primeval dreams are mine to share with those
Who bear my sigil as a hidden mark;
Who praise my horns, which are the crescent moon . . .
My children of an ancient wisdom know
And raise the colours of the wondrous dark.

Psalms and Sorceries

Druidry

Pale moonlight floods the lonely, windless wold.
In misted hour, long before the dawn,
As darkness breathes with mysteries untold

And all the stars within the welkin spawn,
I tread through mist that curls up to my knees.
Around me, shadows lengthen, as if drawn

Across the heath and heather by a breeze,
Flowing towards a site of heathen lore—
A ring of stones where gods were once appeased.

Suddenly, silence lifts from off the moor,
And aerial elemental forces weave
An eerie voice that calls from unknown shores,

Beckoning all the shadows to receive
The wisdom of a holy world unveiled
In eldritch splendour of this solstice eve:

And all the shadows turn, begin to pale—
Like eidolons from some lost lineage,
They pass between them each a glowing grail,

And one among them, priest or archimage,
Recites a rune that is the druid spell
To praise the Earth, and ancient ghosts assuage . . .

Slowly, the vision dissipates, dispels.
Again I walk alone upon the wold,
Now pondering if some prophecy foretells . . .

The windblown mists and vapours curl and fold.

The Ghosts of Hyperborea

Beyond the polar region's death-white plain,
Black monoliths, like giant sentries, seem
To guard the limits of a lost domain
Amid eternal snows and glacial gleam—
Where ghosts, who took strange glory to their graves,
Now walk forever on the winds that rage,
And whisper of weirds from their forgotten age
Before Atlantis sank beneath the waves.

The spirits here were giants in their day—
Great conquerors, whose names were raised in chants
By evil slaves and holy hierophants . . .
But of their chronicles, now none can say.
The bitter, boreal winds that ever gust
Have long-since blown their epitaphs to dust.

Out of Endor

The horned red moon has risen clear,
And evening augurs heresies;
The rites and rituals commence—
And demon principalities
Grow silent momently to hear
Our song of strange malevolence.

Dark shadows rise, and we converse
With emissaries of the shades.
Our awful pacts, by men unheard,
Are signed with black, ensorcelled blades
In sigils solemn as a curse,
And cuneiforms of primal word.

We whisper weird and secret plans . . .
And to the demons offer praise
For giving us the arts that show
Those channels through which spells might raise
The horror of leviathans
That roam the black abyss below.

Ecclesiastical Triptych

I. Relics

Narrow the way, the steep descent
That leads into the sacred space.
Here darkness is a sacrament.
Three black-cowled shapes, at altar bent,
Still sanctify the worship place.

Untarnished in the days that were,
The ornate iron censers rust.
Once clouds of frankincense and myrrh
Arose to keep the cloister pure;
Now incense made of mummy-dust

Pervades the deep penumbral gloom.
The trinity still seem to pray.
They left impressions on the room—
One hears their phantom chants of doom,
The meditations on decay

In reverence to nightmare's nod:
How fervently they kneel beneath
The idol of their demon god—
Each corpse a little open-jawed,
Their oblong skulls, their shark-like teeth.

II. Black Robes

They are as shadows from beyond,
These black robed cenobites who glide
Among the mausolean stones,
Silently, as assassins might
In summons to some horror spawned
In hours of the eventide,

Even as owls and wolves descend
On prey to rend and vivisect.
Scattering viscera and bone,
They make dark art within the tombs,
Hither from hell to all attend
And serve their eldritch analects:

A covenant to keep old ways—
Immersion in a primal rite
Which ends in soft, sepulchral moans
Of awful appetite appeased . . .
The glutted shadows slip away,
Their black robes blending into night.

III. Ladies of the Everlasting Lichen

They wander out *en masse* near vesper time,
A sisterhood embraced by the unknown;
They trail black habits, smeared by mould and grime,
Shambling along the courtyard cobblestones.

One scents these bridesmaids of oblivion
At distance: by a pungent, earthy must;
Then sees that squamous lichens mar their skin
With purple patches and pale ochre dust.

Devout till death, their vows have gone unchanged—
Black jelly lichen seals their lips up tight;
No intimated meanings are exchanged
Between their blank wide eyes of milky-white.

All night they shamble. But as dawn light falls,
The Ladies of the Lichen make their way
Toward the chapel, through the cloister halls,
And at the lichened altar seem to pray:

And as they pray, the lichen-webs that vein
The rotted pews and old iconic art
With greys and greens of creepers, crusts and stains
Begin to pulse, as with a beating heart:

These sisters neither feel, nor see, nor hear,
But with a lichen-mind communicate
Strange peace that hails from worlds unknown to fear,
Where grace and glory grows, immaculate.

The Shrine

The elders of our clan believe the shrine
Has stood here since before the dawn of man;
It broods there blackly, palpably malign—
A place forbidden by a tribal ban.
To whom the shrine was raised remains unknown—
To god or demon, or some nameless saint;
An aura of the darkly sacrosanct
Ensures the eerie shrine is left alone.

In darker ages, there were chosen few
Who therein sought the mystery enshrined;
But only one of them to us returned,
To preach a gospel alien and new . . .
And he and all his acolytes were burned
For knowing things not meant for human minds.

Alastor

There is a spirit wandering through space
Of regions most remote and desolate;
That bound to solitudes, may never sate
An impetus to travel place to place—
From boreal wilderness and weird white wastes
To desert dunes that whisper of despair,
It roams eternally the haunted air
Of ruins and lost realms by time effaced.

The spirit but a sourceless shadow seems
Amid mirages on the sighing sands—
Flitting to caves and dark colossal tombs,
Searching for some unknown among those glooms
And silences that speak of other lands,
Of alien worlds that ancient dead men dream.

Oracle

What were the things you meant to say
Before you left for other lands,
Those distant regions, dim and grey,
To dwell amid eternal sands
That know not night, nor break of day—
That twilight realm without a sun,
The kingdom of oblivion?

Hear you, that we would here receive
The mysteries that you can tell
Of worlds beyond, but few believe?
Hither to us and doubt dispel,
If only for a while to leave
Your house in Hell untenanted—
Come whisper us wisdom of the dead.

Spells

The wind that animates the barren trees
In atmosphere a little crisp and cool.
Dead leaves that whirl alive upon a breeze.
A ring of ripples in a still black pool.

A star that swiftly pulses blue-red-green
In skies as cold and quiet as a tomb.
A covered icon, holy face unseen.
A chamber ghosted by a soft perfume.

The symbol gestured by a wizened hand.
An image frozen momently in flames.
A voyage through an unfamiliar land.
The whispered syllables of secret names.

The thing suggested at the edge of sight.
An incantation of an ancient tune.
The music of a creature of the night.
The forest shadows underneath the moon.

Bats

Past twilight, and the bats emerge
Out of high hollows in the cliff.
Erratic flyers, darkling, swift,
They wing apart and then converge,

A fleet of pointed sails that sets
Out voyaging the ebon sea.
The moon is green; it gibbously
Enframes their jagged silhouettes:

Sharp angles in nocturnal flight,
They glide and arc, they flit and dart;
A swarm of motion, they depart
Like shadows, stealthy through the night.

Toads

Have gathered at the breeding pond,
Enormous, bloated and obscene:
A million mottled sickly green,
All from this very bog were spawned.

Ill moonlight glances off each back.
One rises out of murk, and wet
With slime suggesting fever-sweat,
It blinks, then sinks beneath the black.

Along the banks, their choir croaks
Abysmal litanies, while clouds
Of noxious vapours sting the eyes;

While one great specimen, quite proud
And puffed-up, solemnly invokes
Foul prayers to gods which govern flies.

Night Hags

O dreamful sleeper
    At the door
Of dreamland's steeper
    Untold lore,
Now what reaper
    To abhor
On Nightmare to you rides?
      In she glides

From nether, needing
    Nascent dreams
For outré feeding—
    So it seems;
Amid the pleading,
    Evil screams
As thought and psyche change,
      Turning strange

To mind unwoven,
    Undermined,
By horrors cloven:
    Now a mind
One with coven
    Of her kind,
That knows not dreams, nor light,
      Only night.

Hex House

Off track in twilight I had found the place—
A ruined house in deep, remotest woods;
Alone for centuries it must have stood,
Forgotten like some tomb by time effaced.
Inside, those worm-worn, wooden walls were traced
With cryptic symbols drawn in ash and mud—
And hieroglyphics in black ink of blood
Were scrawled on every inch of surface space.

I shuddered as the evening gathered gloom;
Transfixed, the sigils held me in a spell
As shadows rose from corners of the room
Like spectral emissaries out of hell—
As if that warlock writing had been read
And some dark other's work had raised the dead.

The Driver of the Dragon's Coach

He comes at evening or when twilight falls,
His horses silent, gliding on the night.
And all who witness X themselves on sight,
Knowing he hastens to his master's call
As if a demon, summoned by black mass.
They say his face forever is the same,
That none have ever learned his Christian name—
Thus call him Charon of the Borgo Pass:

For souls his coach collects do not return,
But travel roads where weird blue witch-lights burn
As *he* communicates with wolf and ghost
That guard the ebon gate to Dracul's keep—
Where passengers become unholy host
At feasts for dragons, wakened from their sleep.

The Secret Prayer of Victor Frankenstein

Attend me, gods and daemons that create,
And see my efforts be not evil-starred,
Although the subject's flesh be gallows-marred—
That nerves and tissues shall reanimate.
Gods, grant me powers to exhume his soul
From outer void of untold emptiness.
An empty vessel pours but nothingness;
This corpse needs consciousness, so be it whole.

I will not care if I am deemed insane.
With faith that heeds no false polarities
That stand as pillars of morality,
I dedicate my research in your names
That men might tread where mortals never trod—
A man shall stand before his human god.

Prophecies and Dooms

The Nightmares

"Trois spectres familiers hantent mes heures sombres."
—Leconte de Lisle, "Les Spectres"

I.

Three Nightmares haunt the ruins of my mind
Like revenants that every night return
With bright red terrors, wicked and refined.

At first they followed in my dreams, then turned
To follow me across the wall of sleep—
A strange, invasive species, I would learn

On waking from a dark, abyssal deep
Of dreams to find them gathered in my room
Like awful toys an evil child might keep.

In every corner now, their shadows loom;
At every step I take they're close behind
With awful whisperings, weird taunts of doom . . .

Three Nightmares haunt the remnants of my mind.

II.

In Sleep's dimension, there are stranger things
That rise unreal to live, then dissipate
Like phantoms vanishing on vapour wings.

These Nightmare-things my mind did not create.
They show me dead horizons, seas of gore;
The visions swiftly change, but won't abate.

It is as if my mind were some grimoire
In which the Nightmares scribble evil spells
To conjure images of death and war,

To summon baleful clangors from black bells
That seem a demon choir as it sings
With iron tongues to praise the outer hells.

In Sleep's black mansion there are stranger things . . .

III.

I see the shadows of those things unseen,
These evil visitors that feed my sight
With landscapes most unhallowed and unclean.

A spectral form of psychic parasite,
They burrowed through the doors that are my dreams—
If dreams are barrows, they are barrow-wights,

With eerie voices screeching quiet screams . . .
I do not understand the awful sounds,
Though all these visions speak to me, it seems.

Is it, perhaps, my mind has run aground
On reefs of madness, wrecked on shores of spleen?
Like leeches to my soul forever bound,

I sense the shadows of three things unseen—!

IV.

The colours of these terrors slowly change;
In total darkness, one can clearly see
Pale horrors for dark glories, wondrous, strange . . .

The sky, a slab of jet-black masonry,
I've slid across my roof to seal my tomb.
The Nightmares, tittering so close to me,

Still send me visions through the cloistered gloom,
Gifting me with a true sight to affirm
A truth that only sane minds may exhume:

The world is but an open grave, *it squirms*.
I see it and withdraw, a man estranged,
For those who walk upon the earth are *worms* . . .

The numbers of my nightmares—they have changed . . .

Two Songs from The King in Yellow

I. Naotalba's Dream Song

The yellow fungus thrives and thrives
Like dust upon our lips and hair,
A pallid shroud upon our lives
And souls that breathe the haunted air

Beneath black stars, where we revive
The shadow of our old affair,
Where yellow fungus thrives and thrives
Like dust upon our lips and hair.

No prophet spoke of what survives
The evil wonders waiting here—
This land of wakeful corpses where
Our love would moulder if alive,
Where yellow fungus thrives and thrives.

II. "And All the Black Mould Sings"

You weep, and all the black mould sings;
Our love, my love, it shall prevail.
See, through the window: ghostly, pale,
The moon feeds on our offerings,

And on this night the spirits wail
The mysteries of charnel things.
You weep, and all the black mould sings,
For love, my love, it shall prevail.

For whom, my love, do you rise to hail
As all the chambered shadowings
Seem turned to greet phantasmal kings?
Ah! I must lift your yellow veil—
You weep, and all the black mould sings!

Prophecy of the Green Death

It came to pass as ancient prophets told,
Their prophecies that said the stars were seeds—
That all would see a star-like object grow
In brightness on its path to Earth, then pass,
Transforming all before it took its leave
So that the world would glory in bright green.

And came the comet, glowing weirdly green,
The pale green of a corpse as prophets told—
Though they saw not the comet tail would leave
A scattering of drifting dark jade seeds
That through the atmosphere in waves would pass
Then settle softly on the earth, and grow.

And Earth now witnessed bitter harvest grow
Beneath a sky become phantasmal green:
A virus through all verdant life now passed,
As if the strain in secret whispers told
Each bud and blossom bearing life in seed
To bitter all their roots and fruits and leaves.

And soon the world was full of greener leaves,
But only poison crops in soil could grow
In metamorphic splendor from the seed.
The sun the stars the moon now glowered green,
And in the lurid glow weird tales were told
Of what might come when hunger came to pass.

And soon the days of famine came to pass
As livestock died for lack of grain and leaves;
And weary was the word as it was told
Green shadows on the oceans now had grown—
That all the fish had gills of sickly green,
That rains of emerald spread further seeds.

From fields of famine sown with darkest seeds
The flourishings of carnage came to pass—
Men fed upon each other in the green
While others by their own hands took their leave,
And all the flora never ceased to grow
Through human horrors that remain untold

As all that race, undone by seeds and leaves,
From time did pass so life might overgrow
Their graves with green and silence, as foretold.

Fields of the Nephilim

Once there walked on the Earth a race of giants—
Grim, huge heroes of old, renowned as warriors.
Know then, this is the way they were begotten:
Sons of God, on a star from heaven fallen,
Came to Earth, and they walked among the humans,
Sworded, shielded in otherworldly armour;
Bright-eyed, evil-obsessed, to none beholden,
And they towered above all men, colossal.
Men beheld them in awe, and bowed in terror,
Seeing them seed each town with alien idols
Bearing names of themselves in selfsame likeness.
Men were made to obey, to make oblations
And give gifts to them: gems and gold—and daughters,
So from opposite orders there was union.
From those daughters of men soon issued children:
Hybrid beings of monstrous size and power,
All unconquerable, bred to blood and battle,
And by blood was the Earth made their dominion.
Age on age, and the epochs turned to eons;
God saw all, and beheld abomination
So he whelmed all the world in endless water:
Clouds took form, and the rains came forth from out them
(Until then there was never cloud or rainfall;
Earth was watered by mists that rose from out it).
Oceans formed, and the waves rolled wide upon them,
Washing away all life, save few, the chosen—
But one carried the sap of life within him,
Sap which flowed in the giant breeds before him.
In this way, after untold generations,
Tribes of giants were born as his descendants:

Rephaim, Amorites, Anakim, the Emim
And the Zamzummin formed their many numbers;
These all settled within the land of Canaan.
Dwelling desert remotes, they built great cities;
Men discovered the cities to their wonder
And were covetous—seeing milk and honey
Flowing forth from the fields, that land of plenty.
Blood was given to God upon his altars;
God was gladdened to help men kill the giants—
This had he sought, thus brought that race destruction:
All were driven to death—or deeper desert,
Dying there in the dust of desolation,
Where their chronicles ceased and were forgotten.

Destroyers

We hone the battle-axe and then the sword:
The drums of doom are pounding, hell-hounds bay;
We rise against the darkness of the horde.

For now amid our valley, Death is lord
And clouds of blood cast shadows on the day.
Well-honed the battle-axes and the swords.

We knew the omens. Now we march toward
An avalanche that sweeps our world away—
We rage against the demon-driven horde,

With all our wrath like molten metal poured
In channels through the enemies we slay.
By well-honed battle-axe and witch-blessed sword,

Valhalla's halls await to be explored,
And screaming severed skulls shall pave the way!
We grin before the grim inhuman horde

So gods remember how our thunder roared,
How lightnings flashed and winds blew crimson spray—
Well-honed battle-axes, sea of swords,
We rage against the darkness of the horde.

The Sayings of the Seers

They came to share what others could not see,
To spread the sayings of their analects—
The eyeless visitors from off-world sects
Who sensed with witch-sight things that should not be;
Who spoke of beings that had always been
Outside dimensions limiting our own;
Of truth and wonders hitherto unknown,
That through their sayings all could now be seen.

And men were eager for a higher world:
Those ancient warlocks met with human scribes
To gift their gospels to the chosen tribes—
Then hatred flourished, genocides unfurled
As verse and chapter spoken to enslave
The souls which haunt that world become a grave.

Haunted Planet

On that dim world where *Juggernaut* was lost,
Colossal ruins loom like tombs of gods,
And livid creepers drape their dark facades,
Those thresholds only giants could have crossed.
Beyond, upon an oddly curdled plain
Where once had been a living, plasmic sea,
We've witnessed—with increasing frequency—
Phenomena our sensors can't explain.

We have but theories of what happened there—
Extinction without any fossil trace—
Though gather understanding of that race
When like pale dreams emerged from breathless air,
Gigantic ghosts of alien lifeforms rise
To roam through ruined cities and dead skies.

The Tomb of Wilum Hopfrog Pugmire

In some strange hollow fearful minds defame,
The sentinels of Sesqua keep the path;
One reaches it through circles of black math
To find the obelisk that bears his name.

Here, in the hour twilight creatures dwell
The mossy mound that is their master's tomb,
The rosy shadows blend with purple gloom
And moan before the Night's black magic spell.

Even as he explores dark gulfs of sleep,
Weird spirits conjured out of unknown space,
Like lovely horrors, at his grave increase;

They hear the wisdom of the worms that creep;
And ever watchful, ward his resting place
From those who would profane his dreamful peace.

Lore

In darkest legend was the lore described;
By darker providence it came to me—
A minor demonologist and scribe;
A lowly priest who served the Holy See,
Who at his bishop's scholarly behest
Had sought and found the dreadful palimpsest.

Upon that mouldy human vellum scroll,
In script half-eaten by the worm and moth
And overwritten by a nameless soul,
Were quotes from Eibon and the Book of Thoth
Regarding entities of ancient mind,
That visited this world before our kind.

What followed were the hidden histories
Of immemorial tribes of peoples lost;
Of continents that drowned beneath the seas,
Of arts and knowledge lost to holocaust
That saner minds avowedly disown,
Preferring ignorance of the unknown.

I read the songs by sorcerers of Mu,
Of primal ancestors who sowed the seeds
Their gods had given them when Earth was new
For evolution of a newer breed,
To proffer to the patron gods profound
When they returned again to Terran ground.

Then followed runes that weirdly replicate
The eerie echoes of the Muan verse—
From lords of lost Atlantis, who relate
Their alien creators were a curse;
And witch-kings of Lemuria whose rules
Were reined by greater masters wise and cruel.

Then baleful rites of worship to that race
Described demonic beings from the stars
Who traveled through the gulfs of time and space
From evil planets that no longer are—
For all their suns in chaos had unfurled,
And caused their race to spread to other worlds.

And written were their sigils, signs and seals,
That overlap into an awful scheme—
A map of mystic symbols that reveals
The way to open channels to their dreams
In manners similar to certain spells
That conjure things from out the seven hells.

With growing sense of horror, here I read
They dwell in frozen crypts beneath the sea,
In stasis bearing semblance to the dead,
Awaiting keepers of their prophecy
To raise their race by necromantic tools
And bear dark witness to their wrath and rule . . .

Provided in the text were keys to prove
To any unbeliever's shuttered mind
That all the locks on truth had been removed;
But final proof took seven years to find,
In one black nameless incunabulum
That correlates the scroll's forbidden sum:

I thought myself a man by God adored,
But learned my god was just a wispy wraith.
An apostate, I keep the eldritch lore,
The revelation of an elder faith—
Our world is but an altar in the void
Where souls shall be devoured and destroyed.

Occult Agency

Between the waking world and that of dream,
We are as shadows that may never sleep.
As covert as the secrets that we keep,
Our cult has watched you from your birth, and deemed
To shape your every fantasy; to spy
Through many eyes of minions and deceive,
Manipulating visions you perceive
While crouched upon your chests like incubi.

With subtle sorceries you are coerced.
We ride on death-white nightmares through your minds,
Subliminal as signals in the signs
Of dreamscapes polymorphous and perverse—
By operations cloaked in blackest black
The cards within your tarot have been stacked.

Beddoes: Marginalia in a Cadaveric Atlas

On Night's black mountain, vision comes to me:
The world laid bare, its corpse upon a slab—
And on it, creatures scuttle like pale crabs,
Performing what seems gross anatomy . . .
Whence have they come, to crawl so horridly?
Slowly, as in some charnel-house in Hell,
They coax the Earth's dead dreamers to expel
Their phantom mottos of mortality:

CHORUS OF CRABS

Each blackened planet that becomes our host,
Each floating orb become a happy grave—
So very ripe for research into ghosts!
In mausoleum, catafalque, or cave,
Each corpse so quiet, perfectly becalmed . . .
Unguent applied; now speak, thou well-embalmed!

CHORUS OF CORPSES

To witness Hope become as shibboleth,
The liquefaction of all faith, all love
Dripping towards the cellared sky above!
A dissolution of the fear of Death
Enabled us to face Him—as was best—
While grinning at His scalpel teeth, and jest—!

Agog, I see the scene disperse, like mist
Some demon's pinion swept through and dismissed.

Wraiths

When from the other side we scry
That all your dreams, like bats, have fled
Beneath a strange sepulchral sky,
Twittering with a final dread
Before they fold their wings to die;
When you perceive the universe
As something like a vast black hearse,

We'll come for you in reddish mist
That rises in the twilight gloom,
Then lead you by your naked wrist
To show you where true shadows bloom.
We are as exiles who exist
Like lovers long-since left behind
In mausoleums of your mind—

The source of voices that you hear
Like vatic echoes of the void,
That whisper wisdom in your ear
Of ways your woes may be destroyed—
That lands Elysian are near,
Where all your sufferings may cease.
We offer everlasting peace

Beyond the matter paradigm:
As wanderer through sabled noons
Unlimited by space and time,
Beneath our glowing ebon moons,
Our blacker sun that shines sublime . . .
Self-murder is an act we bless.
Come merge yourself with nothingness.

Methuselah

Relentless, like the wrath of God,
The great epochal cycles turn.
I've watched their motion, rapt and awed,
Seeing all things in time return
To render meaningless all change . . .
All things to me seem still and strange.

Down the dark eons, age on age
I've witnessed wickedness, and wept,
Seeing my kindred on each wage
Recurrent nightmares, for they slept:
False hearts, false faiths, false tongues, false deeds—
From man, abomination breeds.

And now, at last, my own decay:
I watch my children build my tomb.
Weary of evil, weak and grey,
I go to greet a welcome doom,
Leaving the truth of all I've seen:
The human race should not have been . . .

Lord, how I've come to hate them all,
The symptom of the universe!
Heaven, I pray you hear my call
And heed my prayer, a parting curse:
That God on them a deluge sends,
That human filth from Earth is cleansed.

Philomathes and Epistemon

Philomathes. Now that the necromancer's chant is done,
His ceremonies raised in blackest night
And each our funerary rites reversed;
Now that infernal forces circle us,
Their demon forms unseen, abhorred but sensed,
Our dead eyes open as we both await
While void-like cataracts that film them clear;
What say you, friend, arisen out of dust
So recently to re-emerge in Space
And held within the Titan hand of Time,
Girdled about again in flesh and bone,
Or some dark substance that resembles it?

Epistemon. Some old diabolist has done his work.
He has a talent, I can give him that;
The speaking backwards of the litanies,
The same delivered on our fresh turned graves,
Was most impressive, raising up our ghosts—
But incompletely yet: and thus I judge
His art to be imperfect in the end.

Philomathes. How long, like motes, we floated in the void,
And did you see the gates of kingdom come?

Epistemon. I saw not God, nor grasp that interval;
A moment perhaps, or aeons. Who can know?
Time is not measured in Eternity.
But now I'd know our present whereabouts.

Philomathes. My vision is vague, but slowly it restores,
Evolving now a scene, nebulous yet,
As though a greenish veil of fen mist parts:
Surely this is the Earth; though alien ground,

And we sit stationed in a middle place,
Surrounded by a stand of ancient oaks
In wizard shapes, and shadowy their robes.
A blood red moon is glowing like the eye
Of blinded Cyclops; and its lurid gaze,
The lamp by which the night's ensorcellments
Are led in secret by our summoner,
Dimly illumes the savage-purposed place.
Oh God, I do not like the look of it—
The trees, I see them now for what they are . . .

 Epistemon. Savage indeed the reason we are here,
Embodied as ghosts, like echoes out of time
But silenced by a louder, howling host
Of long-damned spirits leagued to hoard revenge.
You say that this is Earth. I am not sure.

 Philomathes. Your sight returns. If you might speculate,
How many brides of Baphomet were burned
Alive and cursing, based upon our words
Which later issued from the mouths of kings?

 Epistemon. As if in answer, vision comes to me:
I see a barren place, a boundless plain
Whose reaches limit out amongst the stars;
And feebly, through a smoke-laced atmosphere,
The tainted glimmer of the wintered sun.
That level surface raises into hills,
And driven into them are many stakes
Upon which hang the countless cindered forms
Of women mostly; children, too, and men
Whose bodies were as fuel, their souls as smoke
For persecution's pyres. An eerie breeze
Is blowing flakes of ash from off each corpse
To fertilize the world with human soot . . .

 Philomathes. A horrid scene I'm sorry you behold.

A word of consolation now, my friend:
I still believe our arguments were sound.

Epistemon. Even as shades and shadows circle us,
I, too, believe the work of God was done:
The hammer falls and nails are driven down.

Philomathes. Since surely we have worked the will of God,
How is it we are here, and to what end?

Epistemon. By all the awful shades assembled here,
Of night-hags, sprites, demonic spirits black,
And women only clad in nature's state
Who wear the marks of witch-cults on their brows,
I hazard answer: I would say their throng
Assumes a supercoven on this night,
Convened for the adoration of the Beast.

Philomathes. This could be just a dreadful fancy formed
Before us in the unformed void—mayhap
As melancholy humours sometimes cause
In simple raving creatures. What say you?

Epistemon. If subtle fluids were responsible
For all this otherworldliness around,
Then surely we were drowned in blackest bile.
Let us not lead away from truth to make
The error of the Sadducees. Behold,
All this before us happens, this is real.

Philomathes. I will embrace the dreamless dark again
When they have done with us what they will do.

Epistemon. I somehow doubt new death shall bring reprieve;
I caught a gleam within the warlock's eye,
A meaning in his cold, sardonic smile:
When they have done with us what they will do,
We will return to awful dumb dead night
For intervals between black sabbath times;

Psalms and Sorceries

Then be recalled, in strange perpetuity,
To face huge horrors we shall soon face here.
A cyclic life-in-death and death-in-life
Is ours for Hell's enjoyments, doom on doom:
A sordid lot; an endless, morbid tale
To go untold to sympathetic souls
Though told throughout the nameless nether realms.
Now hold to faith, be master of the will
So not the deeds that reach us from the dead,
Delivering evil as to break the mind,
Score strange confession from the tortured breath:
Our apostasy, won by force of fiends.

    Philomathes. Below is the abyss; there's nothing above.
The metaphysic sabbath fires burn
As devils grope and lick our hell-bound souls.

The Monstrous Voice

Scylla and Charybdis

Scylla. How fare thee over there, disgusting hag?
Anything new upon that lonely rock?

Charybdis. A scourge of flies, and mites between my scales.
So many mites! At least the day is fair.
What of you, foul thing? Have you any plans?

Scylla. My cave is dank, and reeking with my dung;
I'd clean a little if I could, you know;
Fashion a broom of driftwood and dry grass,
But I've no arms to sweep with . . . What a waste!
I guess I'll seek contentment on the shore,
Sunning myself upon the sun-soaked stones
With all the lazy snakes and lizards there.
But really, I'm a little bored with it.

Charybdis. Ah! I begin to thirst . . .

Scylla. And I could eat,
With many angry mouths to feed. But look!
The skies portend: perhaps a storm; perhaps
A more doomful thing. See how the clouds churn,
As if a goddess some black cauldron stirs,
Brewing a bitch's batch of wrath, no doubt.

Charybdis. Aye, the skies grow darkly, lances of light
No longer glint upon the cobalt waves;
The sea grows shadowed, night replaces day.

Scylla. I often wonder, philosophically—

Charybdis. It matters not. I must now quench my thirst.
My belly, full of glowing coals, it burns;
Nothing is more important than to slake
This urge that thrice per day I must appease.

Scylla. Then go, my counterpart, and drink, drink, drink!
There she goes, sliding her hideous bulk
Into the sea. And now that she's submerged,
A whirlpool swirls, widening ever wider,
Signal to all that Charybdis consumes
The very fathoms from unfathomed deeps.
Gods! What a ghastly bladder-beast is she,
Utterly ugly, horrid to behold,
With flippers for arms and legs; that massive maw
She says was once a lovely human mouth.
It's true she suffers badly of her fate,
But was there ever gloomier thing than she?
Although I doubt her "human" heritage,
I'll find for her a little gladness yet.
She thinks I know not of her parentage
(Some sea-god or another—that's for sure—
With goddess or some other concubine).
It's obvious by how she carries on;
Besides, we monsters sense each other out
Innately—transformations all aside—
But why she tries to hide it—beyond me!
Gods, how she carries on. I've suffered, too;
Once Phorcys met Hecate and they bred,
Spawning all sorts of creatures on the world,
Then left me on this barren rock to rot
After their evil rutting. Boredom bound,
Before the coming of old Charybdis,
I spent long years without much company;
Grotesque, a horror is my only friend.
What's this I see? Aha! All hells be praised,
Here comes a ship! It sails between our rocks
That adjacently form this narrow strait.
But no, it does not sail; the tidal pull
Of the wide water vortex draws it near.

Charybdis! Again you've made my meal,
Sending these sunburnt sailors for my feast!

  Charybdis (submerged). Drink indeed! Insatiate this thirst;
My belly swells like some unsounded void,
Abyssal and bottomless, or so it seems
When this abhorred thirst has swallowed me.
But submarine, I find a brief reprieve
From all that blasted barking from her breasts . . .
Scylla scrapes balefully upon the nerves;
She grates mine down, then grinds them into dust.
A ghastlier thing alive could never be,
Her myriad jaws all lined with many rows
Of shark-like, gleaming, huge serrated teeth;
Her legs are giant, writhing serpent coils,
And snarling, slavering dog heads are her teats . . .
Most loathsome, and the more iniquitous
Between us both, I think—but to myself.
Now what is this I see? Those flailing shapes
Sinking towards the sea-bed—and to me,
Caught in the funnel formed by my huge gulps.
I recognize the taste of human kind,
And see the wreckage of their ruined ship,
Its tumbling cargo, too: clay casks and crates
Spilling stone statues, ornaments of bronze,
And golden things encrusted with bright jewels:
Some are quite lovely; but what use to me?
Let Triton scavenge all those man-made things,
Such treasure can adorn his coral halls.
My thirst is almost sated (for a while);
Meanwhile, the water reddens all around.
I'll rise above, where I imagine much
Inestimable evil going on,
That Scylla vents with crazed malevolence.

Scylla. Your curse unquenchable has sealed the doom
Of one huge human vessel—what a feast!

Charybdis. I saw men sink below, and swallowed some;
It seems the sky ill-omened for that crew—
Fools who would dare the dangers of this strait,
Knowing that mortal peril herein lurks!

Scylla. These men are full of sweet red wine, they burst
Like juicy grapes between my gnashing jaws!
So hast thou slaked thine awful, monstrous thirst?

Charybdis. For a while.

Scylla. I saved you tasty gobbets,
If you'd dine.

Charybdis. I hunger not.

Scylla. I've also saved
Some broken bones. The marrow is quite sweet;
And hollowed, they make little flutes . . .

Charybdis. Enough!

Scylla. This is the good life, Charybdis! A curse
Is a curse, but look, such benefits!
Really, the torments that we must endure
Mean little when our plates have human meat.

Charybdis. And what when all the gorging has been done?

Scylla. Spoiler of joyful moments, off with you!
Waddle and flop the way into your cave,
And keep your counsel to your haggish self!

Charybdis. Only to make you happy, my dear friend.
I'll remove myself to the gloomy dark
Before I'm moved again, by curse compelled.

Eurynomos

"At Delphi, there is a painting of Hades by Polygnotos. Depicted therein is Eurynomos. The Delphian guides say he is one of the spirits of the Underworld, who devours the flesh of corpses, leaving only their bones . . . He is of a blue-black colour, like that of meat flies, and he is shown with bared teeth and is seated upon a vulture's skin."

—Pausanias, *Description of Greece*

The meat-flies serve me with their million eyes;
Through them I see another over there,
Lying alone, all wrapped in cerement cloth.
This one is clean as she could ever be;
I'll drop her fleshless carcass and move on,
Crawling across the hill to get me more.
I'm always ravenous, so it is good
That Hades is replenished frequently.
Here it is, well-hidden among the stones;
I must have passed him many times before.
A recent entry, this one; not yet ripe,
His putrefaction just a faint perfume,
And still a little subtle for my taste.
Perhaps I'll leave him yet; let him mature
Into a fly-blown thing, softer to chew,
A fruit more ripe for peeling sweeter flesh,
Flowering in his pestilential fumes
As all his seeping pus and ichor pools.
His sunken features, appositely pale,
Are oddly mottled yellow-red and black;
He must have been a victim of disease.
The Nosoi must be busy spreading plague;
I've seen a few just like this recently.

Now, as I see no other corpses near,
I'll settle down and chew his fat a while.
While not full-rotten yet, he comes prepared,
Well-seasoned with the bitterest of herbs:
I taste a little insolence and pride;
He's savoury with malice, and there's spite.
His juices would suggest a jealous heart . . .
Undone by envy, this one, I suppose.
How strong his flavours flow, delicious in death!
I'm nearly done with this one.

                    In the end,
They all corrupt with foulness, every one—
But some grow even fouler on this side.
I've eaten bodies hidden very well,
But shown to me by their own spectral selves.
They are the ones old Charon has refused
A passage on his boat across the Styx
For they've received no funerary rites.
A burial is sacred, and completes
The final custom gods on men imposed,
And Hades will not have them incomplete.
Unlucky shades like those have sought me out
Across the quiet plain of skyless gloom,
Leaving a while their brethren spectral throngs
That wander on the darkling river shore,
Sharing a ban upon forgetfulness
That flows beyond, in realms forbidden them.
They come to me in very clever thought,
Thinking to bury proof of evidence—
To make their blameless bodies disappear
In hope of getting on the boatman's barge.
Asking me to remove it from all sight,
They lead me to their silent, ghosted house—

And bid me with all haste inherit it!
I devour their corpse; they go their way,
Thanking me in profusion. I then turn
To call a vulture for my messenger,
Who flies across the vaulted dome of night
To croak intelligence in Charon's ear.
For that is our agreement: deeds done cheap
Against the self to get oneself to Hell
Are impious, screaming for some punishment.
But there is hope.

                Not all are so corrupt
As all these corpses that I must to eat;
My devotees are promising, in ways.
Once, when the mortals knew not of my name,
A man descended to the underworld
To fetch his bride from out the house of death.
Upon his useless voyage to us here,
(When otherworldly music filled the halls
Of Hades, haunting it with eldritch art)
He learned my name by whispers from the dead,
And later uttered it upon the earth.
It took a tiny root; my cult was sown,
And blossomed frightfully, a thing obscure.
Their lot is numbered by a very few:
All outcast men and women, lowly ones
Who live like worms in tunnels of the earth.
They honour me by imitative means,
Performing what could be my holy rite:
Robbing the graves and newly risen tombs
Of liars, blasphemers—and criminals
Convicted by an honest, lawful curse
Some righteous victim once invoked by right.
My devotees go seeking only those:

Gnawing the putrid flesh from off their bones
And lapping liquefaction in the grave.
With foetid morsels filling up their mouths,
They leave behind them yawning, emptied tombs.
I've seen a spectre tremble in despair,
Sensing the things committed on its corpse . . .
So much the better, if it's swifter work,
When carrion overflows all Hell in heaps.
Ungrateful spirit I, if not to share—
They pick some unclean bones from off my plate.

Gorgonum Chaos; or, The Sisters of Medusa

There is a blasted shore that lies between
A waste of waters and a desert waste,
An endless wilderness of waves and dunes:
Ill-gathered and isolate, evil lore
Has builded superstition on that place,
And few have made that wilderness their world.
Not far from where the darkling waters break
In ceaseless rhythmic tumult on the shore,
There is a gorge, dividing jagged cliffs
An immemorial turbulence had hewn.
In that ravine, a constant shadow falls,
Save when the sun in its diurnal arc
Has reached its zenith. Here and there,
Amid huge boulders and the wind-hewn rocks,
Are other stones in human image cast:
So similar their likenesses to life,
Their features wild, in ghastly aspects posed,
Surely their sculptor was a sorcerer
Who had with strangest intimacy known
Her subjects. Beyond those eerie statues
Which men should heed as solemn warning signs,
The rift leads on, narrowing at a bend
Where of a sudden, strong ophidian stench
Pervades upon the stifling, gloom-fed air,
Developing a signal to the sense
That peril lurks from ledges overhead
Which drip with dark pollution of the bats.
In darkness, where the crevasse terminates,

There is a cave, accessible by path
That steeply leads into the cavern's mouth;
The foul mephitic scent is strongest here.
Now, from that gaping portal, something moans:
A guttural sound, as from a growling beast,
Ascending terribly into a wail:

> *Stheno.* Ai-eee! Our mortal sister has been slain!

> *Euryale.* Ai! Ai! Medusa, sister, you are dead!

> *Stheno.* All butchered and grotesque, her bloodied corpse,
Beheaded by the adamantine sword
Athena's servant wielded in the dark,
Before he fled our iron claws and fangs
As we gave chase, in mad futility,
For darkness had concealed him like a cloak,
Thwarting our fair pursuit of Perseus.
Before us here, her gravid body lies,
Martyred before the shrine of motherhood.
The coward slew her in her very sleep,
Taking her severed head, then watched her writhe,
Her limbs still thrashing with an awful life
Even as all her ancient lifeblood ebbed.

> *Euryale.* Low deeds by him, whom deities have deemed
As just, and men will deem as demigod!

> *Stheno.* Already the dead to dead in darkness speak
Of her descent into the nether pits.
In that dim world, removed from life and light,
She'll find a den to haunt in Hell's remotes,
Keeping a distance from all other shades
That roam the regions of the somber realms.
Secluded in the shadows of a cave,
She'll thrive alone on bile of bitterness,
Gnawing the bones and gristle of remorse,
And ever ravenous to taste revenge.

Psalms and Sorceries

Euryale. Most beautiful among the monstrous brood
Of grim primordial gods who govern seas,
She fed Poseidon's appetite for rape
Upon an altar in Athena's shrine—
And for her very victimhood was cursed:
The bright-eyed goddess spurned her, granted scorn,
Seeing Medusa's features fit to hex
By metamorphic magics . . . and now, *this!*
To further outrage far beyond repair,
The vipers—slithering hither to converse—
Now whisper of the goddess's intent
To make Medusa's head an ornament,
A gore-bright standard on her battle-shield.
Upon our kindred will the kindness end?

    Stheno. Wait! Now from afar, we hear of other crimes
Athena instigates against our kin:
Of how her agent, seeking out our place,
Has vandalized our sister sentinels.
He claimed to seek their counsel, then he stole
The only eye between the ancient three,
Leaving them helpless as mere mortal crones,
And ransomed it for rare intelligence.
From them he got our hidden whereabouts—
Then cast their eye into the open sea.
Against the Graeae we can hold no grudge;
Who wouldn't bend to save their sense of sight?
To rectify dishonour and disgrace
Of dread chthonic elders, we will seek
To balance scales with human hecatombs.
Graeae, be glad for givings you will get—
We'll gift you eyes we gather from the dead,
A giant bag of baubles dripping blood
So by your witchcraft you might weave new sight.

All this, directed by that slut divine:
Conspiracy, slaughter, infamy and lies!

    Euryale. Such are the ways of those who make the laws,
But they themselves are lawless and corrupt.

    Stheno. The system earns my loathing and disgust.

    Euryale. But how is one avenged against the gods,
What could we take from them who have the most?

    Stheno. They all are vain, and seek to be adored.

    Euryale. It seems to me they bathe in reverence.

    Stheno. A supplication uttered in their name
Is milk and honey they most gladly drink.

    Stheno. They wallow in that worship, like the swine
In its own filth. To me it seems obscene.

    Euryale. If men were not, no gods would sit on thrones;
They draw all power from the well of prayer.

    Stheno. Then let us stanch that water at its source.
Sister, your mind to me is most well-known;
Even as mine I know it, and I know
That we are sworn against Athena's throne
For all this ruin by her jealousy,
This huge conspiracy against our kind.
A war eternal, rightly, we will wage
Against her powers over this, our world;
Immortals with eternity to plot,
Perfection shall be ours in black revenge—
We'll glut upon the very guilt of gods.

    Euryale. But first to blood relations we attend:
Let us perform the necessary rites,
Then build up a pyre for Medusa's corpse
To send her back to Chaos properly.
The sickly sweet putrescence of the smoke

Will carry far upon a charnel air,
Forming black clouds of bleak funereal gloom
To gather under in the time of grief
While sending signal to the Phorcydes.
When all our awful lamentations cease,
And each of us has filled a lachrymal
With tears of venom, we'll deliver them
In pure and potent evil to the wells
Of human villages within our reach,
So that their blood might blacken in their veins,
Leaving them all aware, but deathly still
As we descend into their streets to seek
The whereabouts of cradles and of cribs,
Then gorge upon their children at the feast
To mark Medusa's honor. Sister mine,
Foam from our human food will overflow
Our jaws, forming a frothy rivulet
That later tribes will think the Phlegethon.
And if a few might safely flee from us,
We'll leave them to their madness, for the mind
Beholden to such horror goes insane.
And then, with dread attention, will we turn
Upon Athena's shrines for sacrifice,
Whereon the very altar of our will
Her priestesses and supplicants will shriek:
For we shall show them why they fear the night—
The black and starless radiance beyond
All light of law and reason: seething hate,
Flowering as a dark morbific bloom
Around the gardens of the sacred fanes,
That strangles as it thrives, and coils around
Athena's idols—bitch, it's you we'd choke.

    Stheno. Abomination and blood upon our breath,
Medusa's sisters execute her will,

Even as out her corpse burst living things
Like sleepers falsely buried in a tomb,
Wakened from dreams of death—the progeny
Begotten by the trident-bearing god,
These spawn that rise from out red sepulchre.

Euryale. Let's peel these web-like membranes from the wings
Of Pegasus to free him to his flight,
Then clean the crimson gore from Chrysaor,
A nephew ours alone to nurture now:
We'll raise him as our murdered sibling would—
Teaching the arts of terror and of doom,
That he might work against the gods, and man.

Children of Hypnos

No healing and no help for life on earth
Hath God or man found out save death and sleep.

—Algernon Charles Swinburne, *Rosamund*

I wake: how happy they who wake no more!
Yet that were vain, if dreams infest the grave.

—Edward Young, *Night-Thoughts*

Dramatis Personae

THE ONEIROI: MORPHEUS, PHOBETOR, PHANTASOS
DIANTHA and EVADNE, attendants to Sotiria
SOTIRIA, priestess of the necromanteion at Heraclea Pontica
ELPIS, suppliant widower
ERICHTHO, the ur-witch of Thessaly

I call upon the Lords of Dream,
    The shadowy and long-winged ones
Who build the imageries that teem
    On worlds that rise without the sun:
You visit silently in sleep
    And stir the visions of the mind,
Inspiring pious souls who keep
    The truth to front, the false behind;
You speak directly to the soul
    And whisper of the will of gods,
Gifting the hieroglyphic scroll
    Of sacred keys to dream facades
Revealing firmament divine—
    Through midnight paths you show the way,
Your lamp the symbol and the sign.
    Hear me, O lords, to you I pray:
From horror please deliver us
    On hearing pious dreamers scream—

Do the dead dream, O Morpheus?
    Tell me, sweet god, do the dead dream?

Children of Hypnos

ACT I

SCENE I.—*A cave entrance near the base of Mount Mausoleum in Erebus. The greenish headwaters of Lethe cascade from the cavern mouth into an illimitable plain of mists and shadows below. Occasionally, spectral entities flit by, wailing miserably. Enter the* ONEIROI. *They are humanoid but ghostly in form, and pulse with shifting lights of every hue and colour, suggesting a supernatural power.*

Morpheus. At last, you two have finally arrived!
Just what in Hades took you both so long?

Phobetor. Impatient Morpheus, I've been at work,
Riding a million nightmares through the minds
Of humankind, shaping the phobias
Best suited to reflect their beastly fears—
Or loves, for that matter. I've sculpted things
Of beauty also, beauties unsurpassed:
Such lovely dreams; oh, yes, such lovely dreams
I raised upon my journey through the night:
Fantastic visions, fine and delicate;
But crude ones, too, barbaric in their cut.

Phantasos. I, too, was busy with my special work,
Creating things of careful shape and cast
In sharpest definition, or in haze
Of veiling mists and vapours, soft and vague,
Combining every element to form
Inanimate objects lending atmosphere
To dreams you populate with men and beasts:
Weaving the weird phantasmagorias
That ornament the dreams of human kind.
What then, O shaper of the human shapes,
Has made you call us here so urgently

To this dank place where our great father dwells?

Morpheus. We're here to wake him, for I need a word
On matters most unusual—

    Phobetor.   You jest!
And know quite well, that when the god awakes
It's only for the gathering of blooms
That make that garden just outside his door—
Those poppies, hellebores and aconites.

    Phantasos. With which he stuffs his gut to put him out
For years or even epochs at a time,
Sealing himself in soft black somnolence
From where he rules dimensions men call sleep.

    Phobetor. Upon his giant bed (more like a tomb—
That Cyclopean slab of jet-black stone
All hieroglyph engraved), he snores and drools,
And all the dribble from his open hole
Becomes a pool surrounding his black bed,
The source of Lethe, flowing sluggishly
To wind throughout the unlit underworld . . .
Few mortals know the origin of it.

    Phantasos. It's full of juices from the herbs he chews,
That bring forgetfulness, oblivion.

    Morpheus. I know all this; to whom is it you speak?
Our father lies forever sprawled in sleep,
A mighty slumberer inside his cell,
As moveless as this mountain over him
That scrapes the darkling skies of Erebus.

    Phantasos. It's best to let a sleeping god lie still.
Are we agreed?

    Phobetor.   All signs say don't disturb.
But tell us, Morpheus, what is this news
That has you summon us in such a haste.

Morpheus. An oddity occurred, and in our name;
It came in form of pious utterance.
You may recall that time when humans built
A temple honouring we Oneiroi.
That group was not for long upon the earth;
Their fane is but an ivied ruin now,
It's crumbling stairs by mosses overgrown,
And nothing haunts its quiet precincts now.
That tiny shrine, which offered us a cult,
I would have thought had passed from memory,
A thing forgotten. Now, an offering
By someone calling out my secret name;
She burned some incense there, and offered blood
Upon the altar which was meant as ours.

    Phantasos. I wonder, how she came to call on you.

    Phobetor. It's dangerous, this influence she has
By holding in her head your hidden name.

    Morpheus. I know not how she got it, but she prayed;
The sad sweet strains of song so softly sung
Affected me in ways I've never known.
I visioned her, so lovely was the voice
That murmured with a haunted eloquence:
As melancholy as November moons
Was all her aspect, when her face appeared.
I felt the strongest urge to answer her;
My thoughts by votive powers seemed compelled.

    Phobetor. My brother by emotion has been moved.

    Morpheus. She also mentioned, as a mild complaint,
The priestess at her local oracle
Has failed to offer any form of help—
Something to do with speaking with the dead.
But I don't wish to step on holy toes
By mucking through the swamps of moral ground;

Involvement with the mortals—save in dream—
Is risky business, as you both well know.

    Phantasos. In mortal life we may not interfere
Outside of dreamscapes in the realm of sleep.
All rights to intervention go to gods;
Even to mention it, right here, right now,
Could raise some eyebrows. Let's tread carefully.

    Phobetor. Apotheosis, once, was nearly ours;
But let's not bore ourselves. To be as gods—
We chose our freedom, choosing not that lot.

    Phantasos. Sometimes, their power holds for me appeal;
Surely, such awesome eminence provides
Some novel, bright amusement, at the least . . .

    Phobetor. I see your logic, leading you astray
And off the cliffs of folly, Phantasos:
Like all great sages, you're completely wrong.

    Morpheus. We've been through this before. To be a god,
One bends oneself to bad dependency.
In dreams we have full reign as monarchs rule;
Why throw that all away? For power's sake?
Let me remind you what the job entails.
It's like some kind of contract has been signed:
"Establish me a cult, and make it grow;
In turn I grow in power—and my priests,
In cultivating my religion's growth,
Shall each enjoy some power over men,
For as above, my priests shall grow below."
The deal is done; both parties play their parts.
Then epochs roll along; the god awakes
To find he's shackled, bound to man's belief.
Strange marriage that, between a god and man;
It is the worst of bad relationships—
But only suicidal gods would seek

To sever it: to them, divorce means death.
And so he's stuck there, serving all his priests,
While looming overhead, one absolute:
Forsaken and forgotten, deity dies
And slowly turns to metaphysic dust.
How many times have we seen that before?

    Phobetor. By seeing to the shutting of our shrine
Before its consecration, we secured
Our freedom from such poor relationships.
They suffer on Olympus, believe me!
Imagine hearing all those sordid prayers
That inundate the thrones with snivelings . . .
You wonder why the poets call gods mad?
It's love and hate that turns them all that way,
Driving the old divinities insane.
Just look at them and how they carry on:
One moment giving favours; at the next
They're smashing humans into smithereens.

    Morpheus. It's just as well we do not share such cares.
Whole worlds are ours alone to rule in dream.

    Phobetor. But even then exists dependency;
Those worlds depend on dreamers dreaming dreams.

    Morpheus. There's that, of course; but let's not dwell on it.

    Phantasos. You re-convince me with your arguments:
No duties of the deities for me!

    Phobetor. So, Morpheus, what say you then about
This woman calling on us with a prayer?

    Morpheus. Well, better safe than sorry. First we'll seek
To wake our father, asking for advice.
It's curious, though, to feel as if compelled
To answer her with some consoling sign.
I could ignore her, but I must admit

Her supplications . . . somehow, they taste sweet.

Phobetor. In suffering exists a sort of fruit;
Beware, however, its strange succulence:
Look how it hooks the gods—they're slaves to it.

Morpheus. Indeed it does. But I seek just a taste
To satisfy this alien urge in me.

Phantasos. You two go on; I'll join you momently;
I sense my latest masterpiece dissolves,
And I would have that dream persist a while.

[*Exit* PHANTASOS, *who vanishes in a flash of kaleidoscopic colours.*]

Phobetor. You lead the way. This labyrinthine place,
Though once our home—it always gets me lost.

SCENE II.—*The mouth of Mount Mausoleum. Pitch blackness.* PHANTASOS
appears. The lights that emanate from his body illumine the cavern walls around.

Phantasos. It's very dark in here; and I forget
Which turn to take when this way branches out.
Does one go left, or to the right, from here?
But then, that right and also left shall fork . . .
A complicated maze! I'll take the left.

[*Continues through the black corridors by taking every left turn.*]

I'll catch up to them soon. They will be pleased
To see that work of wondrous edifice!
I have ensured that dream stays stabilized;
The architecture of my genius waits.
Ah, finally! But wait; is this the place?
This vast black door, it bears the same designs
Upon the gates of horn and ivory.
They must be marks inscribed by father's hand.

This isn't then the way towards his cell;
I've reached the gate that shuts our brethren in,
A place forbidden to us, in our youth.
Well, that was long ago; what does this say?
There is a short inscription written here:
"Halt! Read no further, for these words are keys—
Beyond, the gaping mouth of madness yawns."
Signed, Hypnos. Ah, so better not to read.
What's this? I hear the sound of tumbling locks.
Maybe he could have spent a bit more time
On choosing how to word his warning sign . . .
The door swings open, grinding dismally,
And ancient, humid blackness looms behind.
Indescribable stench! Powerful, foul!
What's that? Another sound, that seems between
The sound of soup that bubbles in a pot
And wavelets lapping on a quiet shore . . .
Strange groans now echo on the cavern walls,
Reverberating with odd cadences.
Is that a voice, or voices, coming now—
The babble of a thousand malformed tongues,
All gibbering nonsense, incoherently!
Weird shapes are moving forward as a horde;
A cloud of shapeless shadows billows out,
All full of colours I have never seen!

[*A whirlwind-like funnel of intertwining shadows, suggesting myriad forms unimaginable to the human mind and exuding emanations of profound psychic horror, bursts like black lightnings from the door and past* PHANTASOS.]

Hello, my brethren! We have never met,
Though I am thrilled to meet your numbers now—
All nine hundred ninety-seven of you!
How strange . . . They do not even notice me.

To be so blatantly ignored—it's rude!
On black phantasmal wings they rise and fly,
Flooding the ebon sky above, and flow
Towards the threshold of the overworld;
They separate, and like black mists disperse
Through gates that pierce the roof of Erebus.

SCENE III.—*The chamber of* HYPNOS. *The god of sleep lies sprawled gigantically amid enormous black pillows.* PHOBETOR *and* MORPHEUS *stand a polite distance from the bed. Enter* PHANTASOS.

Phantasos. It seems I may have made a small mistake.

Morpheus. How do you mean?

Phantasos.   In coming here, I took
A passage leading not . . . directly here.

Morpheus. Just what is wrong with you two? This was home,
And it was here that we as children played!

Phobetor. I think he speaks about that other place
That we were all forbidden entrance to.

Morpheus. So tell us, Phantasos, exactly where
In this dark citadel you found yourself.

Phantasos. A passageway that led me to a door.
Upon its face, inscriptions have been carved;
They look quite like the carvings found upon
The very gates of horn and ivory.

Phobetor. What did they say, those glyphs upon the door?

Phantasos. I paraphrase, but: "Do not enter here."

Morpheus. A warning, then.

Phantasos.   And then, a sort of key . . .

Phobetor. To open the door?

Psalms and Sorceries

Phantasos.   I dare not speak it.
But I will take you there, so that you see.

    Morpheus. Then lead the way into that foetid place
Where all our thousand nameless siblings dwell,
Each monstrously amorphous.

[*They begin to follow the passageways that lead to the forbidden door.*]

                    To behold
That league of inchoate, aborted things
Sprung forth from out our father's darkest dreams—
The gathered gloom of all his illest thought
Seeping and spreading, sucking to the walls
In testament to madness in his mind—
It's not a thing he'd want sane eyes to see.

    Phobetor. The walls that form this tunnel are quite cold.

    Morpheus. And dripping with oneiric residue . . .

    Phantasos. This is the place.

    Phobetor.   The door, it is agape.
Beyond, the cavern echoes its own void.
I take it that our brethren quickly fled
And passed those portals to the overworld?

    Phantasos. It was a strange and morbid spectacle;
But yes, they made all haste in leaving here.

    Morpheus. And straight into the sleeping minds of men.
No living man or woman sound of mind,
Nor even those whose minds are most unsound,
Could bear such horrors, nor would wish to see
So much of madness and the dark macabre.

    Phantasos. But could this little error be so bad?
These horrid dreams, phantasmal after all,
Do not hold substance, they are things unreal.

Morpheus. Their very power is they are unreal.
Can we, or mortals, hold true forms of things,
Or touch an object immaterial?
What substance does the mind manipulate
But immaterial matter: that of thought.
Only the mind may mould a thing unreal,
To give it shape and give it to the world;
Such dreams as these can turn the mind to things . . .
Incubating with awful potencies,
So long occulted in that darkened keep,
They will inspire minds to evil ways,
And drive them where the mouth of madness yawns—
Even as that inscription clearly reads.
Not normal nightmares these, our Nightmare kin.

    Phobetor. From out miasmal cauldrons of the mind,
A nameless legion seeking for a shape . . .
The disembodied, in new bodies born . . .

    Phantasos. Your philosophical monologues affright.

    Phobetor. O brother! by the void of intellect
So often we have witnessed, you have won
From old Pandora that which was her crown!
You take her place, supreme in idiocy.
How feel you, sitting on your lofty throne?

    Phantasos. Enthroned by error; yet, the throne is mine.

    Phobetor. Another reason, then, to wake the god;
He'll have our hides when he has learned of this!

    Phantasos. If I may interject . . .

    Morpheus.   But he is right,
There's nothing else to do.

    Phantasos.   I interject . . .

    Morpheus. Oh, spit it out!

Phobetor.   Just say what you would say!

Phantasos. If we stir Hypnos from his holy sleep,
Perhaps this minor error, which is mine,
We might omit until you've told your piece
About that woman; managing his mood,
Perhaps by sprinkling humour on your tale.
Yes, get him chuckling for a little while
Before all mention of this other thing.

Morpheus. Even when we were children, you were first
To seek deferral of our father's wrath.

Phobetor. Instead of waking Hypnos, why not seek
Some guidance from his brother, also here?

Morpheus. Down there, where Thanatos our uncle dwells,
No visitor has ever been received.
Even our own eyes, seeing through all night,
Cannot perceive in that strange blackness there.
Wearing the very darkness for his robe,
Uncle abides, sequestered in that dark.
He sits before his ebon crystal ball,
Gazing on darker darknesses . . . Who knows
What eldritch horrors he beholds, but he?
His concentration is intense, complete,
And never wavers from that weird black sphere . . .
Dislodged from total focus, who can tell?
He might destroy us for disturbing him.

Phantasos. I doubt he would destroy his nephews.

Morpheus.   Death?
Did Kronos on his newborn children feast?
Best keep in mind just who we're dealing with:
Even the gods abhor him. Let's avoid
All thoughts of calling uncle from his cave.

Phantasos. What avenues are open to us, then?

I must admit some nervousness; this deed
Has opened a dilemma. It is deep.

    Phobetor. At last, my brother, wisdom walks with you.
Alas, there are two issues facing us;
Though one, without a doubt, takes precedence.
Some foresight seems to be most paramount,
We need perspective on futurity—
This thing you have unleashed upon the world
Will lead directly back to us, of course.
The other issue is quite serious,
But Hypnos need not hear of it just yet.

    Morpheus. That oracle our woman mentioned—she
May know a thing or two; she might be wise;
Perhaps a seeress, even. Let us go
And pay them both a visit. Maybe there
Some answers to these problems might be found.

ACT II

SCENE I.—*The necromanteion at Heraclea Pontica. The place is situated on a rocky promontory overlooking the city and its bay.*

    Phobetor. So this is where the hero Heracles
Once dragged the dog of Hades out of hell.
In total terror from terrestrial light
His six black eyes had never seen before,
Cerberus spewed up all his bile and fear,
Which dripped on some pale plant beneath his paws,
Poisoning it, so that it would produce
These aconites that flower all around
In blue abundance. Lovely, hooded blooms!

[*Like tourists taking in scenery, the* ONEIROI *begin walking down a winding goat path towards a cluster of small buildings situated near the cave of the necromanteion.*

Meanwhile, near the bottom of the path, DIANTHA *sings while beating the dust from a rug.*]

The happy worm is most content
When she has meat to chew;
Corporeal her element,
She wallows well in grue.

The happy worm is glad and fat
When she has meat to suck;
Unhappy she, when thin and flat,
As other worms won't—

[*Enter* EVADNE.]

    Diantha. You're back already. What news from the mob?

    Evadne. I've heard odd things are going on down there;
Though what was told was whispered second-hand,
And that within the hamlet off the skirts
Of Heraclea proper.

    Diantha.   Oh, do tell!
The usual tales of wretchedness and woe
Inscribed in catalogues of crime and vice?
Of faithlessness and infidelity,
All forms of gross corruption, graft and greed?

    Evadne. Of course all that; but something other moves
Behind the curtain. Yes, I've heard weird tales.
A woman bit her child upon the cheek
For merely bawling; yes, she chewed it off,
Then tossed the brat, all bloodied, in the drink.
As if awakened, suddenly she screamed,
And those who gathered round her saw her face
Gone white with horror: now she realized
What she had done. Inconsolable now,

She stalks the crowds, imploring to be stoned.

    Diantha. No doubt the brat deserved it. Did it drown?

    Evadne. A fisher saved him. Yet another tale:
Two strangers met for double suicide.
And travellers spread word of stranger things
Beyond the city. Some say holy men
Who gaze upon the heavens to espy
The movements of the gods have seen dark shapes
Descend upon the cities like black clouds,
Then disappear like mist.

    Diantha.   Dark omen, that!

    Evadne. And everywhere there is the talk of dreams
Disturbing folk so that they get no sleep.

    Diantha. Let's hope the illness does not spread to here.

    Evadne. Indeed, let's hope. How is Sotiria?

    Diantha. She's miserable again, with migraine aches.
She hit her potions hard again last night.

    Evadne. All because of one incorrigible wretch!

[SOTIRIA *moans from inside her house.*]

    Sotiria. My blood crawls . . . Are there spiders in my veins?

    Evadne. She's worser than she was just yesterday.
What can we do?

    Diantha.   Murder the offender?

[*Enter* ELPIS, *from the road to the city.* DIANTHA *and* EVADNE *regard her icily.*]

    Evadne. Today has found our priestess indisposed;
Besides, it's for the best you don't return.

    Elpis. Then I'll retrace my steps to here quite soon;

I'll be the judge of when to quit this place.

[*Exit* ELPIS. *The* ONEIROI *round a bend and into view.* SOTIRIA *shuffles unsteadily from her house, displaying symptoms of delirium tremens.*]

    Diantha. More visitors arrive, from up the path.

    Sotiria. Who's that? Tell me, not Cimmerians again;
To suffer those barbarians today . . .

    Evadne. They handle me quite well—

    Sotiria.   They're savages!
What, you'd like to weave us all new robes?

    Diantha. These don't look like Cimmerians to me;
They're altogether alien in their kind.

    Morpheus. Hail! We've come to ask a word of you.

    Diantha. Today has found the priestess indisposed—

    Sotiria. Enough of that, Diantha. Be so kind
To bring these visitors some bread and wine.

    Phobetor. We need no nutritive as mortals do;
Our sustenance is manna made of dreams.
We seek the counsel of Sotiria.

[SOTIRIA *pauses as if checking her memory, and then nods in recognition.*]

    Sotiria. What brings immortals to this holy place?

    Morpheus. In part it was a prayer, in part complaint.

    Diantha. Should we be bowing? Are you all divines?

    Morpheus. Just tell us of that woman coming here
Who seeks your aid, that you refuse to give.

    Sotiria. Well, what is there to say about that bitch?

    Evadne. There is no thing as bothersome as she.
Listless she crawls along in doleful black

Like some grim vision: slow, lugubrious,
Her eyes all red from weeping, and she moans
Incessantly in sorrow for her loss.
This place we call our home has now become
Her place of solemn vigil. She would see
Her loved dead summoned up from hell, a shade.

 Diantha. It's true, that woman pesters us enough
To see her husband's ghost. She's obstinate,
And haunts us every day, at times by night,
Demanding conjuration of her dead.

 Morpheus. Why not perform the service, and call forth
That spirit with whom she would dearly speak?

 Sotiria. We have. It's complicated business, that.
Our efforts have not worked at all on her,
And so we try no more.

 Diantha.   Yet she returns.

 Morpheus. As priestess of this oracle, perhaps
You might relate to us another thing.

 Phobetor. We seek a seer's sight for things foreknown,
Of sights forebanned save from eyes of Fate.

 Morpheus. We understand such power here is had
By those who keep the oracle.

 Sotiria.   I see—
I mean, I understand why you might think . . .

 Evadne. Today has found our priestess indisposed.

[SOTIRIA *gives a disapproving look to* EVADNE, *who shrugs compliantly.*
SOTIRIA *sighs.*]

 Sotiria. O children of that god who governs sleep,
I'm no seer; no prophecies move my lips,
I cannot tell you what the future holds,

I'm blind to destiny, as mortals are.

   Morpheus. What is it that you say?

   Diantha.   We're charlatans.

   Phobetor. The powers of this oracle are false?

   Diantha. I swear by Styx.

   Evadne.   We work a little hoax.

   Morpheus. Describe this operation you perform.

   Evadne. It's older than the hills. Our subtle art
Is based upon suggestion, and some drugs.
We interview the patient to surmise
What they would have the spirits tell to them.
Administering our potions then, they sleep
A sleep that is not sleep, but is a state
Somewhere between a daydream and real dream.
All this occurs in yonder yawning cave
Where we perform the holy pantomime:
Wearing white sheets, our faces smeared with ash,
We dance about them whispering of things
We've understood their hearts most want to hear.
We're practiced at this; never have we had
Dissatisfied suppliants, but now *her*.
Such is our necromantic art, passed down
Among the cults who keep such oracles.

   Sotiria. Initiates in sacred mysteries,
These secrets now you keep in confidence.

   Phantasos. Aha! It seems we join the priestly caste.

   Morpheus. The joke's a good one, wasting much of time.
So tell me, holy one, if one would seek
Authentic artists practicing these arts,
Where would one look?

   Sotiria.   They'd go to Thessaly,

And mingle with the witches in that land.
The old black magic lives and breathes out there;
It's said the mother of their kind resides
In some remote and rocky place, where rites
Unholy and unknown are done by her.

    Morpheus. Then we will visit that far place at once.

[*The* ONEIROI *vanish.*]

    Sotiria. Well that's a thing one doesn't see each day.

    Diantha. Oh, no; I see black veils . . . The plague returns.

[*Enter* ELPIS *from the same direction as before.*]

    Elpis. I see that you're no longer indisposed.
Would you at last perform the sacred rites
In ways that satisfy this grieving soul?

    Sotiria. You are immune to aid from oracles.

    Evadne. But tell us, since you come to us from there,
What happens in the city? Have you seen
Or heard of things . . . that seem not in their place?

    Elpis. If cities by observants are conceived
As living beings in their days and ways,
Then Heraclea's surely lost its mind.
I know not what to call what happens there,
But something morbid and abnormal moves
Through street and square. Its rhythm is quite off,
And everywhere the eyes of maniacs
Are lurking, if one cares to take a look;
All those who've kept their wits about them see
The grimaces of leering lunatics
And smiles of the demented. Things devolve;
It seems the city creeps to greet its doom.

[*Enter the* ONEIROI, *appearing suddenly as if from behind a veil of invisibility.*]

Elpis. By all the gods! What nature of beings
Are these before me? Ah! not natural,
But from beyond it! You must be divines!

Morpheus. Supernatural, yes; but *not* divine.
Though recently, you visited a place
Erected in our honour long ago,
And there you prayed, and made a mild complaint,
Invoking us with old occulted names.
How came you by those names?

Elpis.   The Lords of Dream!

Sotiria. Look at her face—she's capable of joy!

Elpis (to Sotiria). But you, the priestess of this oracle
Can take no credit for my happiness!

Sotiria. Your case has proved unique, just ask about!
So many other visitants we've helped.

Elpis (to Morpheus). I learned them from my father, who was wise,
Descending from a line of holy folk
Who sought to raise that temple in your praise.
He kept an ancient wisdom taught to him,
And taught it to me in his turn, although
That shrine of yours was never sanctified
Before its builders up and disappeared.

Morpheus. The pathos in your prayer affected me,
And thus we've come. What aid that we may give
Remains unknown, for there are boundaries
We may not cross, at risk of crossing gods.
You wish to speak with your dead husband's ghost.
That is a thing that we cannot perform.

Elpis. Do the dead dream? For if the dead do dream,
I pray you mingle two: both his and mine,

So we might meet and speak to make my peace.

 Morpheus. It cannot be. The dead, they do not dream;
Though it is true that death is like a sleep.
Hades has His dominion; we have ours,
The quiet steeps of dreamland, bordering;
A similar darkness builds in both domains.

 Elpis. But help me still, I beg, to find some way
To reach him, and by that set mind to rest.
He left for battles far across the sea.
Since then, I've heard from men who fought with him
That he was killed, but they know nothing more.
Is his grave marked, or does his body rot
A nameless lump, fair pasture for the worms?
It grieves me much to think he's carrion,
A pile of disarticulated bones
All heaped together in some unmarked pit.
This is a thing I dearly wish to know,
And knowing it could put my heart at ease:
At last I could perform the obsequies
That fit his mode of passing, then move on.
It eats at me. I'm lachrymose, alone
And without knowledge which could set me free!
And this is why I first came to this place.
For far and wide, the necromanteion
Is famed for conjurations—where the dead
Rise up to walk before the very eyes
Of those who wish to see them and converse.
But all these holies here cannot perform
Such operations—they have tried and failed.

 Evade. Our mistress did her best with you. Depart.

 Elpis. I think I'll stay right here, at least a while.
The city sours and curdles down below;
A lady feels unsafe alone down there.

Sotiria. It's true, strange happenings are going on . . .
Who knows the cause?

Phantasos.   Well, actually, you see—

Morpheus. Some god or other likely takes offence
And metes out punishment on that account.

Phobetor. It's as he says, as ever is the case.

Sotiria. The truth is right as rain within your words;
But still, it must have been a great offence!
Old Heraclea in a strangeness swims.
And I feel . . . strange. Come ladies, to my room.

[*Exeunt* SOTIRIA *and attendants.*]

Phantasos. Evasive explanation—not the truth?

Morpheus. Since when do we immortals need explain
The things we do affecting mortal lives?

Phantasos. You have a point. We owe them not a thing;
In fact, it seems to me, they owe to us.

Phobetor. How often do they thank us for their dreams,
Without which, they are nothing? Thankless ones,
Who toiling uselessly upon the earth
Have never, in a holy wonder, thought
That dreams are all that drive them to great deeds,
Giving the gift of meaning to their lives?
I much prefer these people when they sleep.
In sleep, their dreams are often fine, unique,
And most amusing—how they entertain!
But moving here among them . . . I'm repelled.

Morpheus. You say this, and these creatures irk me more.
But gather Elpis; soon we will depart,
Before the very ground around us goes,
Dissolved by nameless, formless awful things
That breathe black vapours into every dream.

Phantasos. So you believe the end of man is nigh?

Morpheus. Think on the situation that surrounds.
A Nightmare needs a host. It seeks and finds.
It gropes its way into a consciousness,
Where embryonic forms will soon take shape
As larval movements of disturbing dreams,
All vague at first—vermicular and vile—
Then worms its way till consciousness is cored.
Lairing in a mind, it leaves its spoor
Behind to fester in the sleeping brain,
Which fevers soon, and night terrors take hold
So tightly that the sleeper, when awake,
Shall see those nighted terrors bleed by day.
This Nightmare is a hungry phantom, crouched
In some dark corner of a cooking skull,
Awaiting its meal to simmer patiently,
Savouring ill aromas off the stew.
So swiftly will this black contagion spread
That soon all reason, utterly undone,
Shall be dissolved from off the face of earth.

SCENE II.—*A high promontory overlooking the city. The* ONEIROI *and* ELPIS *stand upon a ledge, observing the night unfold.*

Phobetor. The night on Heraclea now descends,
Its vast soft shadow falling from the sky;
Immersed within the immaterial wave
Of darkness, now the city slowly drowns.
An eerie haze comes creeping low across
The bay's dark waters, strange and beautiful;
And flying shadows, hid by hideous mist
Are flitting like great bats through street and square
As taller shadows from the stars descend.
It's clear what happens now: unhappy fate

For human kind, embraced by horror's hold.

 Morpheus. From city to city now the Nightmares spread,
Their growth is exponential. Man is doomed;
They won't recover from insanity.
What still remains is what the gods will think,
When all the mortal coil unravels, folds;
For madness breeds forgetfulness: the shrines
And temples, emptied of all votaries,
Will echo like the voice of untold tombs
That beckon gods to enter.

 Phantasos.   You're too grave!

 Phobetor. If staring at such ends, would you not think
To take some holy vengeance on the hides
Of those responsible for your demise?

 Phantasos. Incredible, I had not thought of that!

 Morpheus. Uncertainty encircles us like fog.
Some knowledge of our future we must get.
And still, this pious woman fascinates
With strong persistence . . . Strange to be so moved!
Perhaps I start to fathom how a god
Might feel towards those kneeling at his feet . . .

 Phobetor. A visit to that woman might be wise;
That aforementioned witch in Thessaly.
Perhaps her power could be used to bend
A future vision for us; and to raise
Some answers for your new-found devotee.

ACT III

SCENE I.—*Thessaly. Night. A remote coastal region. The moon is bright and full, illumining the landscape. There is a hut nearby; the flickering light of a hearth-fire comes from its window. The* ONEIROI *and* ELPIS *appear.*

Elpis. And where are we, how came we to this place?

Phobetor. This is the soil that long ago gave birth
To sorcery. We've come to Thessaly.
You slept; thereby, our passage was more swift.
We've come to pay a visit over there:
That modest house of thatch and mud and bones,
Where dwells Erichtho.

    Elpis.   I know not the name.

Morpheus. If anyone could help you, it is her.
She is a necromancer above all.
Her ancestors first systemized that art,
And all such knowledge lives and breathes though her.

    Elpis. Is she bad?

    Morpheus.   She owes us ancient favours.

[*A leather curtain across the doorway of the hut is drawn open, revealing* ERICHTHO.]

Hail, mistress of weird magics, stranger things.
We come to seek—

    Erichtho.   I know why you have come.
The stars have spelled disaster in the sky;
Long-wizened to their language, I have read
Of portents and huge prodigies to come.
Last night the moon went black; no cloud obscured
Their hieroglyphic writing from my eyes.
I scried the scroll of night until the dawn . . .
Also, I paid attention in my dreams.
And now the Lords of Dream are at my door!
A pleasant yet expected meeting, lords.
Though tell me—so I'm clear—which one of you
Unlocked the portal Hypnos locked himself?

    Phantasos. It was I.

Erichtho.   Ha! The youngest of the three.
I should have guessed.

    Morpheus.   So tell us how the gods
Will take all this.

    Erichtho.   You worry what will be;
That gods might punish you for emptied shrines,
When madness wipes from human memory
All trace of their religions. You're wondering:
Will we be treated like Prometheus?
Well, have no fear. This changes minor things;
The wheel of fate revolves upon its post.

    Morpheus. Extinction of all human kind might be
Upon us. Nightmares from the sleep god's mind
Are loosed upon them; how could they survive?
Remarkable mutations such as these,
So swiftly breeding in the minds of men
And multiplying numbers of their brood—
Inseminating evil into dreams
So every dreamer, waking, has gone mad—
Must surely spell the end of times for man.

    Erichtho. How is their kind consumed by merely more
Of that on which the human race has thrived?
Without their horror they would be bereaved;
But only for a while—then they'd rebuild.
No, this is not extinction: They'll evolve
To keener killers, fed on chaos, war
And all the baleful brews that feed their hate.
Your misbegotten brethren lead them on
To greater glories and to destiny.
Oh, certainly will be some holocaust
The likes of which before has never been . . .
But if you seek to lessen out your blame,
Then place it on Pandora and her jar:

But notice, how the elder gods refrained
From punishing her impudence. And why?
They wanted her to spill it all! Like her,
The gods have guided you to do such deeds;
They see all things, and therefore plan ahead.
And would you like to know that secret plan?

    Phantasos. Why, yes! A fascinating thing to know!

    Erichtho. Well, I don't know it! But a plan is there,
Be sure of it. This small catastrophe
Is just one step among the many steps
Upon the stairs to some great masterwork—
And I'd behold it when it is complete!

    Elpis. What language are you speaking? It sounds . . . old.
I have not understood a word you've said.

    Erichtho. At last she speaks, the melancholy wife.
I understand the lords have brought you here
Because you prayed to them—as people should—
About a little problem you incurred.

    Elpis. "A little problem?" That is what you call
My situation?

    Erichtho. Well, little or large;
All things of course are relative, my dear.
But now to other things. Come child, come here.
We must prepare you for the ritual.
And while we're at it, lords, if you won't mind
Helping a lady out—fetch me a corpse.

SCENE II.—*In the hut of bones.* ELPIS *and* ERICHTHO *sit beside the hearth fire. A cauldron stands in a corner beside a table. Various dried plants hang from the rafters; clay jars line a row of shelves. A green cat sits in the window; its violet-hued eyes glow eerily in the shadow and firelight.*

Elpis. I've never seen that kind of cat before.
A lovely creature . . . Native to this land?

Erichtho. He hails from regions very far away.

[*A long pause.*]

Elpis. Those women at the oracle were false.

Erichtho. Such is the way, when things get organized.
But there is something to be said for faith
Where none might profit power or from coin.

Elpis. I place my faith before the Lords of Dream,
But what I sought of them they cannot give.

Erichtho. It's true the dead don't dream, believe it, dear.
But dreams may be directed to the dead:
A little incubation, dwelling thought
Upon desired ones, so they might rise
Within the realm where rule the Lords of Dream.
They can devise for you most any thing,
For they are clever in their artifice—
The masters of illusion, fantasy.
Oh, they could bring your husband back to you.
But simulated things are hollow things;
And who would want that, knowing it's not real?

Elpis. I would not.

Erichtho.   Then you're not like most others,
Who crave delusion and distraction most.
Well, you're a sweet one, and deserve my help.
But so morose and solemn! My dear child,
I give good news; in learning it, rejoice:
Tonight you'll hear your husband's voice again.

Elpis. To speak with him for one last time means all.
Erichtho. If last times for eternity could last!
But all is measured by the sands of time—

You'll have until you see the light of dawn.

    Elpis. I thank you for your wisdom and your help,
Your kindness moves me! Tell me, is your name
A word for kindness in your dialect?

    Erichtho. My mother and her mother had my name;
Her mother had it, too; and hers before,
And when the time of motherhood is mine,
My offspring, too, shall keep it—as will theirs.
So shall it be until the ends of earth,
When void of Chaos enters to consume
The world and all within its gathered dust.

    Elpis. Relate to me, wise woman, how you'll make
The meeting happen for this widower.

    Erichtho. That is a very special thing to know,
And rather complicated. Let's just say
The dead crave nothing more than drinking blood.
We'll lure them with it.

    Elpis.   What blood? You mean mine?

    Erichtho. Go to that cage and grab that sleeping babe.

    Elpis. Whose child is it?

    Erichtho.   It does not matter now.
I stole it, having seen the thing you need.

    Elpis. It does not cry.

    Erichtho.   Well, it's been pacified.

    Elpis. It does not stir at all!

    Erichtho.   *Well* pacified,
With milk and honey, and some . . . sweeter things.
Now place it in that mortar.

    Elpis.   Why do that?

    Erichtho. Now place it in that mortar.

        Psalms and Sorceries

Elpis.   It is done.

Erichtho. That's very good, you take directions well.
Now take that heavy pestle and make paste.

Elpis. Have you gone mad? Destroy this little child?

Erichtho. Hurry, there isn't any time to waste!
Don't you still seek the thing you came for, child?

[ERICHTHO *mutters a series of incomprehensible syllables under her breath. A change comes over the countenance of* ELPIS.]

This is the only way! Now do the deed!

[ELPIS *screams in horror; and screaming, proceeds.*]

Erichtho. That is good. And now for the finale.

SCENE III.—*A graveyard behind the witch's hut. The* ONEIROI *are taking turns at digging with spades.*

Phantasos. I rather like that lady; she seems wise,
Much wiser than most witches at her age.

Morpheus. Her wisdom is derived from lineage;
The ages of her line are summed as one.
Her mother was the famous-most of fiends,
The queen of night-hags, evil pure and prime—
Of vicious inclination: calm, yet vile,
Like reptant creatures are before they kill.
Men feared her awesome powers (they still should),
And speculating on her origins,
A few conjectured that she was produced
By some vast accident among the stars;
While others philosophically surmised
Some curse had caused her parents to conceive
The vile conception, evil at its birth.

Your spade uncovers grave cloth. There's the corpse.

Phobetor. Completely rotted through. The head, it lolls
And seems to leer at me as worms pour out.

Phantasos. It's in a very sorry state, but still
Might serve the witch's purpose. We will see.

SCENE IV.—*All are assembled outside in a space between the graveyard and
the hut. Moonlight floods the scene.*

Phobetor. Here is the corpse, fulfilling your request.

Erichtho. But tell me first: was there within the grave
A tablet with a curse inscribed on it,
Or else, perhaps, a figurine of clay
With iron nails run through its little form?

Phantasos. None were uncovered; then again, such things
We did not look for.

Erichtho.   Good that none were found.
They're efficacious things, but only work
If grave invaders touch them—then, look out!
But simple imprecations can be stopped
Before their motions roll upon the mark,
If one has learned the ways by which it moves.
In any case, you three have nought to fear;
I doubt such things could ever work on you.
I'm implicated; all the worry's mine—
But not too much; as many times before
I've cancelled out such funerary spells.
Well, that is that. It's time we got to work.

[ELPIS *gestures at the dead body.*]

Elpis. I want to see my husband, not that . . . *thing.*

Erichtho. That *thing* still has a tongue that it can wag;

He'll serve us as a sort of middle-man.

Elpis. Your meaning has escaped me, I confess.

Erichtho. Imagine Hermes, crossing back and forth
Between the borderlands of life and death
As messenger: like is the role he'll take.

Elpis. You'll animate this corpse to make it speak?
That would offend a person, though he's dead . . .

Erichtho. I might offend his feelings, but the flesh
That made him once a man will be unharmed.

Elpis. It's unimaginable heresy!
I urge you: conjure just my husband's shade!

Erichtho. Well, what did you expect? His spectral form,
Come forth from out a visionary crowd
To glide into your arms with sweet embrace?
Have you provided me with hair, or bones
With just a little meat attached? If so,
A different scene before you would unfold;
But you've come unprepared. I've said my part.
Shall we proceed?

Elpis.   The horror! Yes, proceed.

Erichtho. Then shut your gaping mouth, or else these flies
That gather on the corpse just might go in.
Now smear some blood upon the dead man's lips.

[*Apparently in shock,* ELPIS *is wooden, emotionless, entranced.*]

Elpis. The deed is done.

Erichtho.   Perhaps it's best to push
Your fingers in, and rub some on the tongue . . .
A dab will do.

Elpis.   Again, the deed is done.

Erichtho. Now everyone step back and give me space.

[ERICHTHO *stands beside the body laid out on the ground. She waves incense smoke from a brazier into her face, and commences her invocation.*]

Lovely Hecate, of the roads
    And unknown crossroads I invoke,
In heaven, earth, or sea-abode,
    Pale mistress of the saffron cloak,
Tomb spirit mighty, who revels
    In souls that flower from the dead;
You gift the necromantic spells,
    And taste the blood on altar bled,
The dripping sighs of all who grieve;
    O queen of spiders, who has spun
An ancient spell by which to weave
    A web that might unweave the sun,
You haunt remote, deserted places,
    Devouring the beasts who dwell there;
As governess of nighted spaces,
    Your voice is owl-screech on the air,
The whisper by a moth-wing whirled:
    I call you now, my monstrous queen,
O maiden of the wicked world,
    Hither from graves you walk between
In soft black shadows of the night,
    Pale empress, I beseech you, come:
Attend this holy work and rite
    To lift a shade from Hell's dark kingdom!

[*A faint, saffron-coloured mist encircles* ERICHTHO *then quickly dissipates. Her eyes roll back into her head, showing only the whites.*]

Haigairos, i-iga hai-ra . . .
Kaltos logomatroi-ka-ra . . .
Zaitro-os, o logo-greva . . .
Monomos-votsalg ki som-va . . .

Come forth from shadows, shadow-wearing shade!
Come sip the blood bedewed upon thy lips!

[*The* CORPSE *licks its lips, opens its eyes, and bolts to an upright-sitting position.*]

Ah, yes . . . you like it well.

    Corpse.   How sweet the blood . . .
So very warm . . . I feel . . . as if alive . . .

    Erichtho. Don't get ahead of yourself. You're still dead,
And now a thrall who serves my every whim.

    Corpse. A little more blood, my liege, so my limbs
Might better serve thy will.

    Erichtho.   So drink your fill.

[*The* CORPSE *drains the bowl and sighs with a wet, ecstatic moan.*]

    Corpse. A-a-hhhhh! Verily, I wait on thy command.

    Erichtho (to Elpis). What is the name of him with whom you'd speak?

    Elpis. It's Charalampos, son of Zosimos,
An actor from Miletus, in his time!

    Erichtho. You heard the lady. Read this parchment now,
And then descend, back to the nether pit
To find the shade who answers to that name.
Relate the words to him and then return
With his response—and then your thraldom's done.

[*The eyes of the* CORPSE *close fast as shuttered gates; a moment passes, then the eyes re-open.*]

    Corpse. Master, all asked is done.

    Erichtho.   So please, relate.

    Corpse (to Elpis). I have a message from your man to you,
But you won't like it. Thus the words he spake:

"I wish for you to join me presently;
I have such sights to show you—of a world
Whose wonders are unworldly, strange, profound;
Where beauty, shadow, horror are as one
All intermingled in death's mystery.
We both shall keep our memories and minds,
Eschewing the un-minded dead who say
The waters of oblivion are sweet.
Come to me, dearest, both of us will roam
Where love and loss and fear and hate combine
As one perception pure, ineffable,
Through holy glories of supernal darks,
Where colours of the darkness are revealed."
The message is conveyed. He misses you.
I'll fetch you straight to him, who bids all haste—
With your permission, master.

> *Erichtho.*   By all means.

> *Elpis.* What have you done with me, you hag of hate?

[ELPIS *yelps and faints;* ERICHTHO *laughs. The* CORPSE *moves in.*]

> *Phobetor.* She's gone unconscious from the shock of fright.
The corpse is shambling, quite unsteadily
On bones held up by rotted ligaments
And blackest magic, dragging the waif by arm
Across the rocks and very rough terrain
Towards the worm-wreathed bed we disinterred:
His grave, a door set on the underworld.

> *Phantasos.* I hear a muffled echo; Elpis screams.

> *Phobetor.* At last, her severed heart is mended whole!
Her lawful wedded one now holds her hands.

> *Phantasos.* She doesn't sound too happy greeting him.

> *Morpheus.* It seems she is no longer our concern.

The curtains of the world on her have closed.

Phobetor. The time and space that held them once apart
Collapses on them now; and they shall merge
As shadows blending into deeper shade.

Phantasos. Their reacquaintance has eternity . . .

Morpheus. And one grows used to horror when in hell.

Phantasos. Well, that is that.

Phobetor.   You seem between two thoughts?

Phantasos. Should we observe with firm solemnity,
Or laughter? Really, this is much too much.

Phobetor. These humans prove exquisite specimens
Of folly and amusement. It is well.

Phantasos (to Erichtho). Forgive me; however, I am curious:
Why was that woman's message written down?
It seems to me she should have spoke herself.

Erichtho. I made her write it out. It seemed to me
That she'd fall mute from horror—which she did—
Stunned by the deep red steps that took her here.

Phobetor. You mean there.

Erichtho.   Phobetor the humorist!

Morpheus. Well done, Erichtho, ridding us of her.
We'd not be worshipped by her human kind,
But lord them from the shadowy darks, unknown.
Such is the way that things were meant to be;
A pest within our house is put in place.

Erichtho. I've done as we discussed, within the dream:
Destruction neat and clean, with no loose ends.
For all the pacts we've sealed before, I owe
At least this favour; I repay my debts.
Unwanted summonings—such dreary things!
And she was sure to summon you again

With righteous invocations and appeals.

    Phobetor. Such botheration would become a bore.

    Erichtho. Vexations! Just another form of hex.
We've merely flicked a bug before its blight.
Let's hope she was the last among her kind
To know your secret syllables of name;
How awful to be summoned and disturbed
By worms so far beneath you. Well, my lords,
The rigours of the evening tire me;
'Tis time this sack of meat and bones got sleep.
Remember me in there!

[ERICHTHO *enters the hut and closes the leather draw-curtain behind her.*]

    Phobetor.   A kindly witch.
It's good to have an ally on this side
Who'll gladly grind the gears of grisly change.

    Phantasos. I feel as if a lesson has been learned,
But have no clue to what the message was.

    Phobetor. I think it means, dear brother, we'll return
To doing things without disturbances
As we have always done since time began.

    Phantasos. This makes me glad, and I'm reminded now
A special dream I made awaits on you!

    Morpheus. Then let us go and see this special dream.
For me, I've seen this woken world enough.
But let them worship which old gods they may,
Or any gods who may usurp the gods.
The secret influencers of the world
Still rule their dreams from darks of Erebus.

    Phobetor. Let's watch this plague of nightmares run amok,
Infecting every mind to be insane.
For now, it seems to me that Phantasos

           Psalms and Sorceries

Has done more good than bad when he released
Our morbid brethren from the foetid cell:
The unhinged mind, unhinging as we speak,
Will be like dough that we manipulate—
Much easier to mould than minds once clung
To reason. I see much potential now.

 Morpheus. The rational is like a rock we lift
From out a garden that we must to plough.

 Phantasos. We'll cast a veil across each sleeper's eyes,
And feed them imagery of our design.

 Morpheus. Their reason always holds them back in dreams.
Without much recourse to the rational,
We'll give them worlds of wild-eyed wonderment.

 Phobetor. Forgotten gods will die; forgotten dreams
Will merely sink into the memory.
Deep in the ocean of the unknown mind,
They'll never lie completely dormant there.
To be forgotten seems the best of things:
The death of gods, ascension for the dreams.

 Morpheus. The irreligious, softened souls of men
To us are golden, pure and malleable:
Each mind an ingot in our treasure trove.
If we can keep the secret of our names,
Obliterate all trace of them from earth,
We'll be in fine position to become
The master movers of the human race . . .
I see a future time where we surpass
All godly powers: when they're gone or dead,
The holy houses just forsaken homes
That sink within the creeping desert sands.
All buried in the quiet dust of doom,
When gods are long-forgotten fairy tales
That even mystagogues have all forgot—

Or teach as stories from corrupted text—
A land of milk and honey shall be ours,
And we will sip and sup their sweet demise.

   Phobetor. Man must forget our names; beyond occult
From henceforth must our names forever be.
By this, our manufacture, we'll ensure
They can't distinguish real from the unreal,
And lord them with illusion. It is good.

   Morpheus. Unknown, unseen, we will increase our rule,
Though men know not to whom to sacrifice—
For holier things than gods shall reign the earth.

Notes: The "Song of Elpis" and the prayer of the Thessalian ur-witch are inspired by the Orphic hymns to Dream and to Hecate. The necromantic scene in Act III draws from the sixth book of Lucan's *Pharsalia*.

Name key: Elpis = "Hope"; Diantha = "God-flower"; Evadne = "Good and Holy"; Sotiria = "Salvation."

Acknowledgments

"Alastor," *Spectral Realms* No. 4 (2016).

"Bats," *The Ladies of the Everlasting Lichen and Other Relics* (Mount Abraxas Press, 2019).

"Beddoes: Marginalia in a Cadaveric Atlas," *Vastarien* 3, No. 1 (2020).

"Black Robes," *Hypnos* 4, No. 1 (2015).

"Cernunnos," *The Audient Void* No. 1 (2016).

"Children of Hypnos," *Children of Hypnos* (Raphus Press, 2020).

"Destroyers," *Skelos* 1, No. 3 (2017).

"The Driver of the Dragon's Coach," *Spectral Realms* No. 10 (2019).

"Druidry," *The Ladies of the Everlasting Lichen and Other Relics* (Mount Abraxas Press, 2019).

"Eurynomos," *Spectral Realms* No. 10 (2019).

"The Ghosts of Hyperborea," *Spectral Realms* No. 4 (2016).

"Gorgonum Chaos; or, The Sisters of Medusa," *Weird Fiction Review* No. 8 (2017).

"Haunted Planet," *The Audient Void* No. 3 (2017).

"Hex House," *Fungi* No. 22 (2015).

"Ladies of the Everlasting Lichen," *The Ladies of the Everlasting Lichen and Other Relics* (Mount Abraxas Press, 2019).

"Lore," *Black Wings V,* ed. S. T. Joshi (PS Publishing, 2016).

"Methuselah," *Spectral Realms* No. 11 (2019).

"Naotalba's Song," *Cyaegha* No. 13 (2015).

"Night Hags," *Penumbra* No. 2 (2021).

"The Nightmares," *Spectral Realms* No. 8 (2018).

"Occult Agency," *Spectral Realms* No. 2 (2015).

"Oracle," *Spectral Realms* No. 6 (2017).

"Out of Endor," *Weird Fiction Review* No. 6 (2015).

"Prophecy of the Green Death," *Dreams and Nightmares* No. 106 (2017).

"Relics," *Weird Fiction Review* No. 7 (2016).

"Rune," *Spectral Realms* No. 3 (2015).

"The Sayings of the Seers," *Spectral Realms* No. 5 (2016).

"Scylla and Charybdis," *Weird Fiction Review* No. 9 (2019).

"The Secret Prayer of Victor Frankenstein," *The Ladies of the Everlasting Lichen and Other Relics* (Mount Abraxas Press, 2019).

"The Shrine," *Weirdbook* No. 31 (2015).

"Spells," *The Ladies of the Everlasting Lichen and Other Relics* (Mount Abraxas Press, 2019).

"Toads," *Spectral Realms* No. 9 (2018).

"The Tomb of Wilum Hopfrog Pugmire," *Spectral Realms* No. 11 (2019).

"Wraiths," *Vastarien* Vol. 1, No. 1 (2018).

www.ingramcontent.com/pod-product-compliance
Lightning Source LLC
Chambersburg PA
CBHW071139090426
42736CB00012B/2164